Prison Possibilities Corrections Coaches

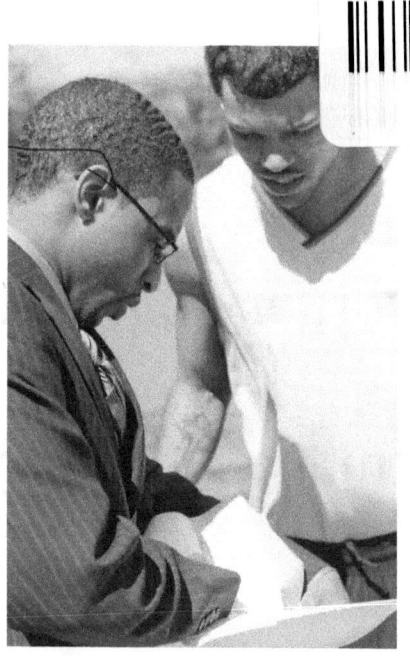

Concept

Rev. Mike Wanner

Copyright Rev. Mike Wanner, February 25, 2017

Selected Images Used by License

Table of Contents

Introduction 4
1 - What Is Corrections Coaching 5
2 - Why I am Writing This Book 7
3 - Correctional Officer Careers 8
4 - Individual Facility Setups 10
5 - Why Reinvent Corrections Officers? 11
6 - The Way to Start 13
7 - Correctional Officers Please Consider 14
8 - "Prisoners Can Contribute and Evolve 18
9 - What Rights Would a Prisoner Be Willing To Trade for What Benefits? 19
10 - And Why Might A Prisoner Care? 20
11 - And Why Might a Correctional Officer Care? 21
12 - What Might a Correctional Coach Do? 22
13 - What Is a Prison Dialogue Series 24
14 - "Acknowledging the Invitation" 26
15 - What Happens Next? 27
16 - Some Topics For You To Consider 28
17 - The Pope Went To Prison 30
18 - Thank You 32
19 - Don't Worry Ever 34
20 - Resource List 35
21 - Angels Please Prayers 37
22 - Private Channeling 38
23 - Reverend Mike Wanner 39
24 - Addendum 41

Introduction

I invite every reader to consider the role that you perceive for the correction officers. Prisoners do not have freedoms and they interact with the corrections officers as one who has been convicted of a crime and is in the presence of the correction officer against their will.

As taxpayers, we in the greater community have an interest in how this relationship works. Our tax dollars are paying for their time together and incarceration is a huge expense.

Conflict does not help anybody and the complications of conflict can hurt us taxpayers by costing more. It seems that I always get back to money and the reason for that is we need an objective measure to look at these situations so we can stay out of the traps of emotionality.

Proper investigation of our options could find that there are options not yet considered. What could we do differently that would have a result that is more positive progressively?

There is a perfect balance between kindness and being diligent in a situation. I invite you to a creative reevaluation of the position interchanges that go between prisoners and corrections officer with the hope of improving the experience for both and creating a dynamic team that resonates at a higher vibration for the good of each of them, their fellow colleagues, the whole facility and the community in general. Giving and receiving are reciprocal so let us raise the bar and the results.

1 - What Is Corrections Coaching

A family doctor treats patients in many ways that include prescriptions, treatment, surgeries, counseling and referrals. Surgeons mostly do surgery.

Correctional Officers primarily keep people in jail and in control. Corrections Coaching could be an upward progression for correctional officers to grow their skill and their service to prisoners, facilities and the community.

The upgrade to coach status would include a utility for the prisoners, facilities and the communities that is new and multi-dimensional. The new role would include the use of skill to help the prisoners, facilities and the community by embracing a peaceful sentence serving and/or a realistic path to rehabilitation and release if they both work to make it possible.

This may not be right for every community and there may be some resistance to the concept. That position is part of the process of re-evaluation which is needed to improve prospects for living inside and/or rehabilitation and/or release.

There is not a clear path to the rehabilitation that I am proposing but the only thing that is abundantly clear is that we are not now being successful enough in that area.

Correctional officers are more familiar with most prisoners than any other contact within the system. That familiarity with sufficient time and opportunity can be a great asset in understanding the motivations of prisoners and discovering all the partnering potential for cooperative effort and benefit.

Skills developed toward coaching could have an immediate impact towards more positive interchanges between the prisoners and the correctional officers. Over time, the officers can begin to discuss things that the prisoners may like to hear.

Human dynamics can be slow but given opportunity, reciprocity can be a powerful reward for kindness. Better relationships can offer better options and it could occur that trust develops further and trust builds further still.

Let's continue to develop ideas about the little things that could make a difference in the relationship between the jailed and the jailers and everybody else involved with either group of people. I believe that little has changed for a long time and it may be time to analyze a lot of the standard operating procedures.

Lessening the density of intensity within an interchange can lead to more productive cooperation that can change the foundations, relationships and future possibilities for all.

Disclaimer

I am not involved with prisons or prisoners but am sharing what is coming to me in an effort to spread understanding and trigger conversation that can be helpful. It may be that the idea may not be helpful to certain facilities and groups and communities.

The hope is that the conversations triggered will be helpful to the overall system and that new leadership skills can take the system to a higher level of understanding and service to the individuals during their time within the walls.

2 - Why I am Writing This Book

I hope that this book continues the work started by my other books and continues to enhance the lives of Prison Employees, Prisoners, Taxpayers and the Families of Each of these groups.

As I have been writing my early books on the subject of Prisons, the complexity of the process has been amazing to me.

The books that I have previously published so far about the prison situation are:

Angel Raphael Speaks Volume 4: Angels, Addicts, Alcoholics & Prisoners – Oh Yeah!
Angel Raphael Speaks Volume 5: Prisoners Caring for Alcoholics - Australia In Miniature Projects Intro
Angel Raphael Speaks Volume 6: Prisoners Caring for Addicts - Australia In Miniature For Addicts
Prison Jobs Now: Providing Care For Addicts And Alcoholics
Angel Raphael Speaks - Prisons (A small Kindle only book)
Contained Care Communities: Concept
Australia In Miniature Projects
Prison Possibilities Dialogue Series: Concept
Prison Possibilities Dialogue Series: Volume 2 Dialogues
Prison Possibilities Dialogue Series: Volume 3 Dialogues
Prison Possibilities Dialogue Series: Volume 4 Dialogues
Prison Possibilities Dialogue Series: Volume 5 Dialogues
Prison Possibilities Voluntary Exile: Concept

3 - Correctional Officer Careers

Some folks might think that a goal of my books is to reduce the number of correctional officers in the system. While there is some truth there in the long view, the most important part is to change the careers of some correctional officers who might choose to upgrade themselves in to a higher level of service and pay.

I have no direct influence on the pay anyone receives. Common sense would indicate that Correctional Coaches who help reduce incarceration, violence, and recidivism would evolve to a value that is worth more to the community than correctional officers who are more traditional jailers.

Correctional Coaches who have enough time to understand and quantify the human dynamics of each individual will be well positioned to recommend the alignment of people and events. Harmony and respectful interaction with prisoners can also help contribute to peace within the whole prison community.

For sake of consideration, the concept that comes to my mind is a potential realignment that could begin to change the system by having a corrections coach become the great intervener in the reevaluation of who performs in a predictable enough way to qualify as the best candidate for release.

The caveat that comes clearly to mind is that this would all take time but the time it takes will be valuable to the greater community as the life enhancement can socially enrich the quality of life for all prisoners and corrections staff and the families of them all.

Correctional coaches could be the wise ones who can reconnect families, and save children from being the child of a convicted prisoner for longer than necessary. Ex-prisoner probably trumps prisoner in the eyes of the kids.

The question that comes to me is "What would be the value increase of a corrections coach over a correctional officer if s/he could impact the system by reducing a segment of population in his/her supervision through reevaluation and alignment with programs that could build skills and set prisoners on a real path of rehabilitation and positioning for release?" I do not know that answer.

The value of these skills would be better set by those within the system. Also, the coach or officer title and responsibility could vary by assignment within different types of facilities.

A steady progression of these developments is desirable to increase safety and decrease conflict. The realignment of programs can improve community living and provide quality enhancement of rehabilitation opportunities.

A coaches resourcefulness could influence the interchanges within a whole facility and provide a public relations level of peace that may be new and refreshing to the families of the incarcerated.

4 - Individual Facility Setups

There is a certain resistance that is natural when one is required to do things in a prescribed way that may make little sense to the one doing the thing. This pattern can lead to the persistence of resistance.

Coaching will not be for every correction officer or every facility and that is fine. The variety of options can be helpful to all.

I have already written many dialogues that can offer ideas of possible changes for residents and their families. I absolutely believe that savings and improved quality of life are compatible.

Please understand that not everyone will embrace every change and that is totally compatible with the suggestions.

I believe that those officers who choose to consider coaching may be in a position to enhance understanding and options for residents. We all need to talk things over with someone who knows the nitty gritty and can offer some perspective from time to time.

It may be hard to understand what exactly I am saying here because I am not using absolute examples. The coach idea includes two way communication so that coaches may be able to understand more and use their influence to establish a network of communication so there is new awareness of the things that can make a difference at all levels of the organization. Understanding is a real step toward healing.

5 - Why Reinvent Corrections Officers?

Corrections Officers are the interaction representatives for the residents and the facility and to some degree they are at risk every minute of every day because they work in a real up front and personal way with those incarcerated. The risks at hand are real but there is also a sense of risk in the energy of the place where they do their job.

The place energy is absorbed from the people who have occupied the space and those who occupy it now. Every occupant has thought energy and a residue from all can remain and pollute or bless the space.

Every occupant can also change their negative thought energy to a positive energy and a residue from that positivity can remain and bless the space at the time of the thought and some or all who occupy it in the future.

I invite every corrections officer and every resident to observe everything as it is better for you if you bring in every little shift of positive potential and release every bit of negative energy that you see. Consider that you are an energy sponge.

Sponges can be clean and nice or they can carry bacteria or a negative energy that is detrimental. You like the sponge can be refreshed and released through cleansing.

Correction Officers may see abuses of many kinds and it is important to help them cleanse themselves from energies and memories that can drop their vibration and increase their stress.

A simple prayer of invitation to the Divine can cause a shift quite quickly.

I would like for the day to come where these new coaches are appreciated in the way that will increase their safety, standing, income and potential to help the residents whom they serve. The energy interchange between coaches and residents can influence their personal peace in ways both understood and not.

The goal of all my writing is to enhance the position for all so that purpose and peace and respect are present on a consistent basis. I would like to see that prison populations diminish but not anyone's job. Over time all fresh vacancies can be rebalanced somewhat as replacements are reduced somewhat. Ideally over time unexpected alliances can be inventive beyond anything suggested here.

That may sound contradictory but I would invite you all to visualize an improved future whereby the status is not to fight with the residents but to help them develop the skills they need to be rehabilitated. If every corrections officer' job is upgraded to a kind of resident enhancement representative, we could easily impact recidivism because the new skills have helped make it possible.

Improved working relationships can also save costs by reducing medical care and pain and suffering. Whoever you are, please consider writing about the changes that you would like to see.

Even though some prisoners may not be able to send their message where they want. They can share it with correction officers or coaches and start a bit of positive energy.

6 - The Way to Start

Like all the books in my prison books series, this book will be deliberately brief for a number of reasons. The intensity of the ideas and thought streams that are coming to me will serve best if they can be interactive and there needs to be enough space to separate concepts so they can be considered.

Moving too fast will be problematic and shift to a complexity that does not serve anybody. Clarity is the goal and that is enhanced when the concept being considered is large enough to focus on but also small enough to not be lost in the process.

A large part of the complexity of every organization is analogous to a tree, where eventually everything matters. When you have a sick branch, the tree will be eventually effected.

When you have a sick tree, the branches can be impacted much quicker because the nutrients for the branches flow through the tree to reach the branches. (This concept is shared for conceptualization only as I have no forestry experience but you can let me know if I am wrong. No worries.)

Using a house analogy, the foundation supports the walls that support the floor above and then the walls above progressively until the roof is finished. We need to put on the roof so that everything below is protected down to the foundation.

I have shared the analogies above and will bring up some example in the following chapters but then you can add more and more so the Reinvention of prisons blossoms.

7 - Correctional Officers Please Consider

Greetings:

Thus far, I have written this as a book but now I shift to a letter style as I want to explain my perspective. In 2013, I Started channeling Angel Raphael.

A Prison Minister consulted with me about her work after I had channeled the first seventy or so messages and after that came some fourteen messages about prisons that were interspersed with other messages. The messages were mostly contained within a block of four messages sets (About forty messages.)

I asked if the block was significant and if I was to publish them separately as a single topic message set and the answer was yes. I published a tiny little kindle book called Angel Raphael Speaks Prisons and released it on Kindle and also included it in a paperback called Angel Raphael Speaks Volume One.

I continued to channel on the requested schedule and later received another eight messages about prisons interspersed with Other messages. Included in that was a particular message in message set sixteen that I was not thrilled to receive.

"I asked Mike to Step in to Prison Energetically

I have asked Mike to get the address and location within a prison of a designated space so he can visit energetically and receive feedback for us. Whether he will have time, interest or opportunity to do this will be interesting to see. As he writes this, he is not thrilled with the idea. We are already consuming a lot of his time." ARS16

No I wasn't thrilled and I really did not want to listen. I already had a lot to write and was struggling to keep up with what I felt compelled to do. Time continued and in 2016 as Part of the Introduction to *Angel Raphael Speaks Volume Four: Angels, Addicts, Alcoholics and Prisoners – Oh Yeah!* I wrote:

"…Recently I was brought to Addiction as a focus of my writing as I see so much of it during Pastoral Rounds at the Hospital.

I just completed a book called *Angels Are Always Around Addicts and Alcoholics* and I did not realize that the completion coincided with a news media production called *Generation Addicted.*

The problem is enormous but the answers are few.

This morning the Angels are talking again to me a lot and I received new insight about turning lemons to lemonade.

While everything is still fresh I will work at integrating the vision, the previous messages and some new perspectives that need definition before words begin to make sense and be conceptual.

This book is about documenting all that along with a fresh integration with what came before."

Since then I have written ten more books about prison and now I am addressing you.

Before all this and after Vietnam, I returned to Sears, Roebuck and Co. in Philadelphia and later was an efficiency expert there. Whenever I did a Time Study, I always consulted with the supervisors and employees in every department that I studied. The wisdom from the frontline workforce was always spot on and simplified my work.

Since I have been writing about prisons, I seem to not see the frontline workforce opinion standing out with the obvious viewpoints to pursue. I feel that is a travesty and I hope that this book can trigger a new level of excellence that is built on the wisdom that the correctional officers know.

Of course, institutional scenarios are difficult but I feel that great problems can be solved if we the larger community can tap in to the wisdom that is there. I can imagine that the likelihood of an outsider opening the conversation is remote.

So, I will share a little that you might be able to use. The Addiction book mentioned earlier is downloadable in a pre-publication format for free (Save Page As) at the webpage http://www.AngelRaphaelSpeaks.com/aaaaaaa/

On that same page, there are tabs for Addict's Prayer & Alcoholics Prayer which can be downloaded and branded with your prison's name. If you have Non-English speakers, there is a English Medical History Form there also for Non-English speakers that may help during language emergencies.

Even if there is no acceptance of these ideas that I am sharing with you, you can read up about coaching for free at your local library and include skills in your work that may just show that you care and add a layer of safety to your job.

In the next chapters, I share also the first two dialogues that I share with the public in the *Prison Possibilities Dialogue Series* because you might just want to share those ideas with the people you supervise so they interact optimally and set themselves up for release.

8 - "Prisoners Can Contribute and Evolve
[Dialogue 1]

Each facility has different rules about the rights and movements of Prisoners. I would encourage each prisoner to consider participation to the full extent of their interest, ability and freedom.

Knowing the rules is an important part of all things in which a person participates. Patience will serve prisoners well if they will wait until the time that comments are invited. You may be surprised to what degree participation is welcome and even desired.

Please know that prison staffs can be most helpful when the people they are interacting with act in a peaceful way. I invite you to be aware of the way that others may perceive you and how putting your best foot forward can help everybody.

Human nature is to be reciprocate appropriately so that respectful behavior is reciprocated with respectful behavior. I invite you to realize that patience can continue to serve you well over time.

Please pay attention and see what you can do that will make a difference in small ways. Little changes can add up over time and create new options for all participants.

I have been amazed at the fact that almost always someone will notice changes and ask why. Why leads to further conversation and further understanding and the expansion of possibilities."

9 - What Rights Would a Prisoner Be Willing To Trade for What Benefits?
[Dialogue 2]

Prisoners have rights that are protected by the U. S. Constitution. Do you know all your rights? If you have someone dear in prison or jail, you may benefit them by learning what their rights are. There are even some rights before prison. Inmates have some rights to be free, from inhuman conditions that may be seen as "cruel and unusual" punishment.

The laws are old and complicated and I am not qualified to interpret them but therein I think may lie some need for updating or modernization. Yes, it seems that the Americans with Disabilities Act does apply but so do some highly restrictive narrow rules. Yes, they are entitled to adequate medical care also.

And the list goes on but the questions I ask is what laws could be changed to allow prisoners to permanently waive rights.

Releasing institutions from compliance with law is not allowed but changing laws to allow institutional freedom could allow prisoners to surrender their rights and prisons to save money and taxpayers to be taxed less.

The question flows from the original Angel Raphael Speaks Message.

"Prisoner Surrender of Rights

Those interested in any of the concepts shared could also consider surrendering of some rights to further the benefits to the governmental unit. ARS11"

10 - And Why Might A Prisoner Care?

Why would a prisoner want to surrender rights? If there is something in an offering that gives the prisoner opportunities that they do not have then they might be very agreeable to waive some rights they are unlikely to use.

So many people think that Law is permanent but it is not. The only thing needed to change a law is an Amendment to the original law according to the appropriate authority.

Prisons have to follow the law but free citizens can campaign for legal reform and that can change laws. Changing laws takes a lot of time so laws are not changed on a whim.

Periodically it is wise to review what is the law and update to reflect the current will of the people. Nothing motivates like money and the state of the national fiscal affairs are a mess so people are suffering for lack of government funding.

Seems like a logical time for change motivated by frugality, common sense and taxpayer interest. In the process of reassessment, we could discover that some processes are both too extreme and too costly to keep.

Common sense will prevail and keep the prisoners most deserving of incarceration. Some changes may be very practical and help prisoners most deserving of freedom to exit and put their lives back together.

Voters can ask their representatives to update laws and reduce sentencing based on reasonable rules. Freedom is wonderful!

11 - And Why Might a Correctional Officer Care?

I would expect that correctional officers, like police, are most concerned with returning to their families at the end of the day. The motivation for doing the work is to fund the needs of the family.

Safety is very important and you never know what can happen in life and even more so in the corrections profession. Your safety and the needs of the family can be very motivating and growth of your skill set and potential can also provide more impetus.

You may have heard the proverbial wisdom from anonymous that declares "What goes around comes around." That may help make you even more aware. Caring about others can have others caring about you and that can make a big difference.

The energy of your workplace can be challenging also so stress can be a factor that cannot be easily seen. I have written about that and have a whole website about it called http://www.StressReleaseCoach.com. Please visit for some free ideas on stress reduction.

I also have a website called http://www.Create-A-Prayer.com that can help with feelings of disconnectedness. In the addendum, I will add a prayer that I wrote for Emergency Service workers in the book
Emergency Medical Kindness In The Cradle of Liberty: Big City - Cracked Bell

12 - What Might a Correctional Coach Do?

The options could be endless but you are subject to supervision so the process needs to be consistently developed in an authorized way. Just like in the dialogue referenced above, patience and discernment are valuable tools to use.

The things that you see and learn every day can be grist for the mill of your creativity. So many people give up on positions that are challenging while others thrive by using the issues that come up as challenges that can be overcome to take themselves and many others to a new level.

I understand the frustration of having limited immediate options but the most important thing is to persist on a path that resonates with your ability to keep going and keep evolving. Writing has been my tool.

I think that a big thing for prisons is the same challenge that our whole society is having and that is the management of emotional reactivity. There are problems in the neighborhoods and similar problems in the prisons.

I am sure you know that addiction to drugs and alcohol are a problem and I have been writing about that but few listen. Before that I wrote about healing and few listened to that also but some people were helped.

I persist and I invite you to do so also and the most important part of that is to stay positive. I have some questions for you and the correctional officer community. Can You help? If you want to help, keep reading.

In the next few chapters, I will post some content from the *Prison Possibility Dialogue Series: Concept* Book specifically for you and other correctional officers/coaches.

The next chapter will be titled What Is a Prison Dialogue Series? And it will be from Chapter 1 of *Prison Possibility Dialogue Series: Concept* Book.

After that, the next chapter will be titled Acknowledging the Invitation and it will be from Chapter 3 of *Prison Possibility Dialogue Series: Concept* Book.

As I have been writing my early books on the subject of Prisons, the complexity of the process has been amazing to me. I would not describe the changes in process as adequate and the more I read, the less impressed I am with the process but at long last I have some perception of a way that might help but there is no certainty.

We need Objective Productive Dialogues about Enhancing the lives of Prison Employees, Prisoners, Taxpayers and the Families of Each of these groups? You are wisdom holders that we need to hear from. {Dialogues can become Policies}

After these chapters, I will propose some Dialogue Topics that you can consider and write about. Create as many other titles as you like on your own.

I encourage you to publish the articles yourself and submit to news media and politicians and also send them to me at ReverendMikeWanner@aol.com if you would like me to consider publishing your possibilities. You can be Anonymous.

13 - What Is a Prison Dialogue Series
[From Chapter 1 of *Prison Possibility Dialogue Series: Concept*]

With this writing, I am starting a structured approach to fracture fear with a quite arbitrary format for a topic of depth that may be pivotal to the quality of life for generations to come.

Incarceration has become a problem for this nation and the intensity of the subject is almost impossible to understand. Fear is a terrible thing and when it gets hold of the thought processes of many, it can create a far more dangerous monster of community fear. Rampant insecurity stifles the expansiveness of thought that could create a platform of security for possibilities in secure nations.

When the nation most adept at fairness feels threatened then our ability to serve the greater good is stifled. Every time that fairness is stifled there is a concentration of possibilities that are delayed, postponed or eliminated.

This may sound insignificant in the greater scheme of things but we would be wise to take a bigger view. When we understand that little frustrations can also stifle the satisfaction of helping for those who start an effort, we begin to see that could cause less initiatives and less willing helpers.

Helping others is a simple pleasure of life that brings abundant satisfaction in a free society. Losing these precious opportunities is not helpful and causes a waste of that which we have precious little, time.

Reasonable people could step up and bring their genius to discussions of practicality and those who give permission could get published by me. Writers are cautioned that if I do not agree, I will not publish but I am looking for ideas that make sense for everybody. I know that I do not have the answers, my question is, DO YOU?

I encourage all readers to consider writing your own ideas about new incarceration models. Many who are reading could have much more impact than I and I encourage you to do that.

Realistically as I am writing, I know that I am over 70 and the likelihood of my ideas making a difference is remote. You, however, are likely younger and can make a serious impact.

Ask on High and follow the guidance. Those after us will be able to thrive better if we do our work now.

Please be bold and respectful and spread the ideas of possibility. I also encourage you to write separately in addition to or in place of anything that you share to or with me.

If you have the interest to help people, you can be successful. The goal here is to help a lot of families who have been impacted by many prison circumstances so that new options that are safer, fairer, kinder, gentler, and more efficient can serve our society.

14 - "Acknowledging the Invitation"
[From Chapter 3 of *Prison Possibility Dialogue Series: Concept*]

"The way to acknowledge the invitation is to respond to or create a Titled Dialogue page outlining the premise of your title so that new dialogues or dialogue responses can be submitted to enhance or counter the initial dialogue. Brevity and clarity of thought is paramount.

There are so many variables that we need to triage thought somewhat and group areas that need action. Pivotal to this effort will be the avoidance of blame because the evolution of what now exists is not easily assignable as participants over the years were acting in response to implementation of the best of limited options and we need not waste more money that does not help current citizens.

Participation is invited to both create and respond to the ideas that are needed to bring change that can impact the lives of those individuals (and their families) who live or work in prison and/or those who are influenced by the shortage of government funds because of the money being spent on prisons.

Responses submitted to me are invited in a particular format to make certain that the responses are similar enough to be easily compared and organized. I hope to be able to publish responses in sufficient numbers to help make a difference.

The desired format is a single Page Configuration >200 words <220 Words, in a 6 x9 book format with all .5 margins, Title Font 20 Pt. Times New Roman, Body Font 14 Pt. Times New Roman. Adherence to the desired format will go a long way to simplify the process for me. Thank You."

15 - What Happens Next?

I will read responses and hope to be able to learn from what is submitted. Please consider sharing your expertise without any blame because pushing against others is usually less productive than teamwork.

Your submissions could be anonymous if that serves you. You could also submit segments for me to consider and write about. If you want your name published or not, tell me specifically.

Really important is specialty knowledge which may be helpful to reset parameters around sentencing guidelines and/or share ideas that may be buried somewhere in antiquated laws.

Trying to understand others and everything has been huge for me during my whole life. I am now able to listen and discern but I am one person and readers like you are needed to listen and discern also.

I lost my dad at age eleven so I empathize with the children of prisoners who feel the loss of their dad like I did. Children of prisoners have an additional loss as they have an association which complicates their lives.

They deserve to be embraced in this concept so that they can get some quality ideas offered to help simplify their challenges. They have not been sentenced directly but their lives are impacted by the system. You can help keep their focus positive.

16 - Some Topics For You To Consider

I had ten more pages of topics to consider but I abbreviated the list so you could have a hint of my concept but also be free to hear your heart proposing the right ideas for you to share.
You yourself and you by yourself can hear very specific things that you could work at to improve and succeed at. I invite you to invite guidance and process with your genius and experience.

Some questions to start with:
How Can You Help Prisoners to Contribute and Evolve?
As a Coach, What Seeds Would You Plant?
What Could You Write that would be Write Might?
What Laws Do Not Make Sense?
What Logic Would Make Law Changes?
Do Prison Prayer Teams Make Sense?
What Idea Do You Have for Rehab Enhancement?
What Could Make Prison Safer for Seniors?
How Can Prison be Safer For All?
How Can You Encourage Light at The End Of The Cell?
What Skills Do Your People Have?
How Can You Use The Antidote To Addiction?
Prisoner Communication Enhancements?
How Can You Be Patient and Effective?
Can You Increase Communications and Safety?
How Can You Increase Freedom For Taxpayers?
How Can You Up Positive Spin in Greetings?
How Can You Up Mental Health in Prison?
Prisoners to New Lives of Service?
Don't Give Up. Start Over!
Share A Bit of Unknown Proper Wisdom That Might Help
Writing Matters But Publishing Is Public

Path To The Exit Created By Prisoners
Profits From Some Can Provide Benefits For All
Societies for Children of Prisoners
Societies for Legal Reform
One Do-Able Step at a Time
Manufacturers Advisory Board
Dialogues for Multiple Jurisdictions
Inventors Analysis Teams
Concept Developments
Lifers Have Nothing to Lose but They Can Give A Lot
Public TV About Prisons
Clearing The Evil of Yesterdays - A Chop to the Mindset
Throw Out Mental Garbage
Can We Have Control and Cost Savings?
Triage Risks for Tranquility
Opportunities To Investigate
Prison Freedom Art
Prison Graduates Community
Community of Independence
Prisoner Counselors
Release for Credentialed Types By Service To Associates
Jail Sections Done Like Disney Where The Kids Can Visit
Clearing House of Exit Possibilities
Streamline Prison Change Efficiency
Prison Writing Literary Guilds
Prison Retreats For Executives - Spare Cell City
Hate Ain't Great – Toxic Yes. Don't Get It On You
Legal Prison Sales Enterprises Can Bring Life & Lift
Rebuilding Prison Rehabilitation

17 - The Pope Went To Prison

While that sounds like a joke setup, it is the truth. Pope Francis visited the Curran-Fromhold Correctional Facility which is about twenty minutes from my house.

The Pope's visit to Philadelphia and the World Meeting of Families on September 22-27, 2015 was quite a remarkable event for Philadelphia. The visit was well covered by the media as it highlighted inclusiveness.

I hope you can use that visit as inspiration to be inclusive also. You are in the position to accelerate inclusiveness by balancing potential and possibility.

Time Magazine has a transcript of his remarks according to the Vatican Press Office. See the whole talk at http://time.com.

I listened to the whole speech attentively and the part that moved me was:

"........ This time in your life can only have one purpose: to give you a hand in getting back on the right road, to give you a hand to help you rejoin society. All of us are part of that effort, all of us are invited to encourage, help and enable your rehabilitation.

A rehabilitation which everyone seeks and desires: inmates and their families, correctional authorities, social and educational programs. A rehabilitation which benefits and elevates the morale of the entire community.

Jesus invites us to share in his lot, his way of living and acting. He teaches us to see the world through his eyes. Eyes which are not scandalized by the dust picked up along the way, but want to cleanse, heal and restore. He asks us to create new opportunities: for inmates, for their families, for correctional authorities, and for society as a whole.

I encourage you to have this attitude with one another and with all those who in any way are part of this institution. May you make possible new opportunities, new journeys, new paths.

All of us have something we need to be cleansed of, or purified from. May the knowledge of that fact inspire us to live in solidarity, to support one another and seek the best for others.

Let us look to Jesus, who washes our feet. He is 'the way, and the truth, and the life'. He comes to save us from the lie that says no one can change. He helps us to journey along the paths of life and fulfillment. May the power of his love and his resurrection always be a path leading you to new life."

Thank You Pope Francis

18 - Thank You

For Considering These Ideas

And
I
Look
Forward
To
Reading
Your
Sharings

19 - Don't Worry Ever

Ever

It Does Not Help!
Prayer Still Does!

Prayer Resource http://www.Create-A-Prayer.com

20 - Resource List

Distant Healing Sessions (or Join Mail List) – Write To mikewann@voicenet.com

Books by Rev. Mike at **www.Amazon.com**

Veterans Healing Six Pack
1. *Trauma Healing Options for VA Hospitals: Help for Veterans to Own Their Healing and their future.*
2. *Trauma Healing Action Steps for Veterans: Help to Start Healing*
3. *Trauma Healing Action Steps for Veterans: Empowerment*
4. *Trauma Healing Action Steps for Veterans: Forgiveness*
5. *Trauma Healing Action Steps for Veterans: Thought Freedom*
6. *Tea For Veterans: Welcome One Home*

PTSD Power Pack:
1. *The PTSD Project: Turn Pain To Power*
2. *PTSD & Soul Retrieval: Putting One Back Together*
3. *PTSD & The Purple PAD: Calling all Scientists and PTSD Patients*

Angel Raphael Speaks Volume 1: Take Courage! God Has Healing in Store for You!
Angel Raphael Speaks Volume 2: Take Courage! God Has Healing in Store for You!
Angel Raphael Speaks Volume 3: Take Courage! God Has Healing in Store for You!
Angel Raphael Speaks Volume 4: Angels, Addicts, Alcoholics & Prisoners – Oh Yeah!
Angel Raphael Speaks Volume 5: Prisoners Caring for Alcoholics - Australia In Miniature Projects Intro
Angel Raphael Speaks Volume 6: Prisoners Caring for Addicts - Australia In Miniature For Addicts
Reiki Journaling from Japan
Reiki Is Alive: God's Great Gift
Four Parts to Healing
Distant Healing: We Are All Connected
Stress Release Energy Work: How To Cope

Does Reiki Love Heal Cancer?
Group Consciousness
Salute To Philadelphia VA Medical Center: Thank You
Reiki Transcript for Reiki 2 & 3 Channels: Dr. Usui Is That You?
God Bless Kindle & Amazon
Puppies Are Different From People
If Your Dog Dies
Toy Guns Are Obsolete
Great Spirit Made Children With Red Skin: AND
The Cage of Fear: Is Not Locked
God Made Children Red, Yellow, Brown, Black & White: Greet Each Child With Kindness
Emergency Medical Kindness In The Cradle Of Liberty: Big City – Cracked Bell
Angels Are Always Around Addicts and Addicts: Help Is Near Now! Invite It In!
Angels Are Always Around Addicts and Alcoholics: Volume 2 - Tools To Help Re-Light Your Life
Prison Jobs Now: Providing Care For Addicts And Addicts Controlled Care Communities Concept
Prison Possibilities Dialogue Series: Concept
Prison Possibilities Dialogue Series: Volumes 2,3,4,and 5
Prison Possibilities Voluntary Exile: Concept

Little Books at Kindle.com by Rev. Mike:
English Medical History Questionnaire For Non-English Speakers
English Language Helper For Non-English Speakers
Wise Wonderful Women Are The Well Of The Family
Answers for Test & Research: Dowsing Power
Crisis? Reiki! Baby? Reiki!
Bible References For Healing
Angel Raphael Speaks – Prisons
Angel Raphael Speaks – Veterans
The Saint Off Interstate 95

Angel Raphael Speaks through Rev. Mike Wanner.
Please visit Facebook.com Angel Raphael Speaks or
http://www.AngelRaphaelSpeaks.com

21 - Angels Please Prayers

Addict's
Angels of Healing Selected
Help Me to Stay Directed
Come To Me From The Sky
I Am Ready to Succeed Not Try
If I Don't Invite You In
I Might Not Win
I Have Been Lost For Too Long
Help Me To Stay Strong

&

Alcoholic's
Angels of Healing On High
Help Me to Stay Dry
Come To Me From The Sky
I Am Ready to Succeed Not Try
If I Don't Invite You In
I Might Not Win
I Have Been Lost For Too Long
Help Me To Stay Strong

From

http://AngelRaphaelSpeaks.com/AAAAAAA/

22 - Private Channeling

Angel Raphael Speaks is a series of free messages that are channeled through Reverend Mike Wanner for the Highest good and Highest Healing of all concerned. They are available on Amazon, Kindle, Audacity and http://www.AngelRaphaelSpeaks.com

Many questions arise about Reverend Mike doing private channeling and he does help with that so e-mail him. Reverend Mike is available world-wide as a psychic channel, emotional release facilitator, spiritual energy practitioner & teacher, and public speaker. He looks forward to meeting you soon!

Email - mikewann@voicenet.com   215-342-1270

PRIVATE SPIRITUAL READINGS/channelings or Spiritual Healing Sessions: Telephone or in person. Rev. Mike is available for private, one-on-one intuitive sessions with you, his Guide Family, and your Guides. He helps by offering clarity on emotional situations about your life, your purpose, your spirituality, and the release of stuffed emotions and cellular memory.

Connect to the love of your Guides today!

Contact Rev. Mike for an appointment.

Sessions available:

Spiritual Readings
Angel Channeling
Distant Reiki Healing
Distant Clearing of Stuffed Emotions
Distant Clearing Cellular Memory
Distant Clearing Energy Blockages
Distant Clearing of the Chakras
Customized needs
Mastermind dowsing responses to yes/no direction finding   questions.

Rev. Mike is a facilitator of healing. He brings you and the Divine together so that you can align with the Divine and have a great time and a great life.

All healing is between you and God, as it should be. Go ahead and start without Rev. Mike. Visit his prayer site http://www.Create-A-Prayer.com. Take the first step NOW.

23 - Reverend Mike Wanner

Rev. Mike Wanner started his metaphysical and ministerial studies with Reiki in 1993 and has studied seven styles of Reiki in the U.S., Japan, Canada, Denmark and Australia. He is certified to teach. He became certified to teach Integrated Energy Therapy in 1999 and co-taught the first IET class of the new Millennium. Mike began dowsing in 2001.

Ordained as a Metaphysical Minister of the International Metaphysical Ministry and an Interfaith Minister of the Circle of Miracles Ministry, Rev. Mike practices and teaches spiritual energy therapies in the Philadelphia Area.

Rev. Mike holds ministerial degrees from the University of Metaphysics and the University of Sedona. He is a Pastoral Care Associate of Aria - Frankford Hospital. He taught at the National Academy of Massage Therapy and Health Sciences.

Rev. Mike was a faculty member of the Medical Mission Sister's Center for Human Integration's School of Integrated Body/Mind Therapies in Fox Chase, Philadelphia, PA for twelve years.

Rev. Mike is licensed by the teaching of Intuitional Metaphysics to practice Spiritual Healing and Scientific Prayer. Mike is also a Prayer therapist.

Rev. Mike was elected in 2007 to the status of "Fellow of the American Institute of Stress."

In 2008, Rev. Mike became a practitioner of Coincidental Recognition as he incorporated the CoRe system in to his spiritual healing practice.

In 2009, Rev. Mike trademarked a new healing process called Quantum Quatro! Subtle Energy System Support®.
In 2011, Rev. Mike joined the outreach program known as the Health Advantage Group.

In 2012, Rev. Mike became a Certified Professional Coach by The Master Coaching Academy and Joined The Personal Empowerment Group.

Prior to his metaphysical, ministerial and coaching studies, Rev. Mike worked for Sears Roebuck and Co. while in High School and after graduation until he joined the U. S. Air Force in 1965. He returned to Sears from Vietnam in 1969 and stayed until 1978. His final Sears assignment was as an efficiency expert in Methods - Operational Research and Development.

He volunteered with Burholme Emergency Medical Services from 1969 and is still a Life Member and Board of Directors Member. He started a private ambulance company in 1975 and worked professionally in the field until 2001 when he devoted his full attention to real estate investing, healing, coaching and writing.

www.ReverendMikeWanner.com

24 - Addendum

Prayer Suggestion
{From Chapter 15 in *Emergency Medical Kindness In The Cradle of Liberty: Big City - Cracked Bell*}

Prayer Suggestions For Police, Fire, Ambulance, Paramedics, Medical Practitioners, Emergency Service Workers, and Correction Officers

God Almighty

I/We recognize you as the source of all good, all healing, all wholeness, all wellness and all support for your offspring in all matters.

I/We unify with your Divine Will and strive to serve your children in all their needs with the same dignity and respect that you do. We appreciate your direction, guidance and protection as we go out to love and nurture all your people in their time of need.

I/We claim our highest skilled functioning under your guidance and our ability to hear the things to do, the words to say and the seeds to plant. I/We claim the healings we will see today are now optimized as this claim is declared and we claim all this or better now.

I/We accept that the optimized care of those in need is started, increased and fulfilled now.

I/we offer my/our sincere Thanks to you Dear God AND SO IT IS!

www.ingramcontent.com/pod-product-compliance
Lightning Source LLC
Chambersburg PA
CBHW061233180526
45170CB00003B/1274